IMPROVING RELATIONS AT WORK

IMPROVING RELATIONS AT WORK

Personal Techniques for Professional Development

Elwood N Chapman

KOGAN
PAGE

First published in the United States of America in 1989 by Crisp Publications Inc, 95 First Street, Los Altos, California 94022, USA.

This edition first published in Great Britain in 1989 by Kogan Page Ltd, 120 Pentonville Road, London N1 9JN.

British Library Cataloguing in Publication Data

Chapman, Elwood N.
  [Winning at human relations: Improving relations at work: personal
  techniques for professional development.]
  1. Organisations. Personnel. Interpersonal relations
  I. [Winning at human relations].   II. Title
  158′.26

  ISBN 0-7494-0061-7
  ISBN 0-7494-0062-5 Pbk

Typeset by the Castlefield Press, Wellingborough, Northants.
Printed and bound in Great Britain by Biddles Limited, Guildford.

Contents

Preface

The relationships you create and maintain with others, whether in your career or your personal world, should be treasured. When relationships are healthy, open, fun, and mutually rewarding they can enrich your life far beyond material possessions. Good relationships will sustain you in hard times.

But interpersonal human dealings are fragile and demand tender loving care. Even when they seem strong, they can never be taken for granted. Those who become skilful at creating and maintaining positive relationships enjoy more successful careers and happier personal lives.

The primary purpose of this book is to assist readers to build and maintain strong, healthy relationships that will enhance their careers. A secondary purpose is to help readers avoid becoming victims when relationships deteriorate.

Although the emphasis is on career or working relationships, all ideas, principles, and techniques can be applied to one's personal life.

Elwood N Chapman

About This Book

Improving Human Relations is not like most books. It has a unique self-paced format that encourages a reader to become personally involved. Designed to be 'read with a pencil', there is an abundance of exercises, activities, assessments and cases that invite participation.

The objective of *Improving Human Relations* is to provide guidelines that will help a reader to understand the importance of developing and maintaining positive human relations both at work and at home.

The book can be used effectively in a number of ways. Here are some possibilities:

- *Self-study.* Because the book is self-instructional, all that is needed is a quiet place, some time and a pencil. By completing the activities and exercises, a reader will not only receive valuable ideas, but also practical steps for self-improvement.
- *Workshops and seminars.* This book is ideal for assigned reading prior to a workshop or seminar. With the basics in hand, the quality of the participation will improve and more time can be spent on concept extensions and applications during the programme. The book is also effective when it is distributed at the beginning of a session, and participants work through the contents.
- *Open learning.* Books can be sent to those unable to attend training sessions.

There are several other possibilities that depend on the objectives, programme or ideas of the user.

CHAPTER 1

The Importance of Human Relations Skills

Most employees underestimate human relations

More careers have been damaged through faulty human relations skills than through a lack of technical ability. Many people are technically knowledgeable but have no idea about human relations, because they are unaware that simply knowing *how to do a job is not the key to success.* To produce results, most of us depend on others and this requires knowing *how to work with people.* Before this can be done successfully there are many human relations skills to be learned and practised.

Some people underestimate the problems that can arise from poor human relations. They persist in concentrating on their own output and ignore the fact that they are part of a complicated team structure which can only operate efficiently when human relationships are given proper attention.

To be successful in terms of human relations it is essential to maintain good relationships with all members of an organisation, from fellow workers to superiors. Communication must be open and healthy. The quality of any relationship will influence the productivity of each individual.

> When Jessica got her first office job she concentrated almost entirely on the accuracy and quantity of her work. Soon the level of her productivity was higher than any of her six fellow-workers and she made no secret of it to others. Did Jessica receive a compliment from her supervisor? Yes, but along with it, she was firmly reminded that she was part of a team and 'broadcasting' her output was causing resentment and damaging the productivity of the others.

Despite her excellent abilities, Jessica demonstrated that she had not learned to balance technical skills with good human relations. She had not learned that her dedicated efforts to achieve personal goals could have a detrimental effect on the work of others. She was blind to the larger picture that involves building and maintaining good relationships with both fellow-workers and superiors.

HUMAN RELATIONS PRELIMINARY TEST

Although human relations skills are not as easy to identify or quantify as technical skills, they are extremely important in your career progress. The more you practise positive human relations, the less colleagues and superiors will misinterpret your goals and the more supportive they will be.

Twenty human relations skills are listed below. *Only tick off those you practise on a daily basis.* This exercise will demonstrate why it is difficult to be regarded as good at human relations.

I consistently:

☐ Deal with all people in an honest, ethical and moral way.

☐ Remain positive and go-ahead even when working with others who may be negative.

☐ Send out positive spoken and other signals in all dealings involving other people, including on the telephone.

☐ Refuse to be involved in any activity that might lead to victimisation of another person.

☐ Build and maintain open and healthy working relationships with everyone at work. I do not have favourites.

☐ Treat everyone, regardless of ethnic or socio-economic differences, with respect.

☐ Work effectively with others regardless of their sexual orientation.

☐ Permit others to restore a damaged relationship with me. I don't hold grudges.

☐ Maintain a strong relationship with my immediate superior without alienating fellow-workers.

☐ Am a better-than-average producer while contributing to the productivity of fellow-workers.

☐ Refuse to initiate or circulate potentially harmful rumours.

☐ Maintain a good attendance record, including being on time for work.

☐ Show I can live up to my productivity potential without alienating fellow-workers who do not live up to theirs.

☐ Acknowledge mistakes or misjudgements rather than hiding them.

☐ Refuse to allow little quibbles to grow into major upsets.

☐ Am an excellent listener.

☐ Maintain a good balance between my home life and career so that neither suffers.

☐ Look for, and appreciate, other people's good points.

☐ Keep my business and personal relationships well apart from each other.

☐ Make only positive comments about those not present.

SCORE ☐

(Score five points for each box ticked.)

A score of 70 or above indicates you are practising a substantial number of recognised human relations skills; a score of under 50 suggests a review of current practices may be in order.

The nature of human relationships

The most objective way to view human interaction is to concentrate on the relationship itself (consider it to be a channel or link between people) and try to forget the personalities at either end. When you concentrate on the relationship rather than worrying about personalities, you can be more objective.

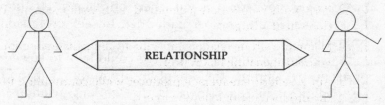

RELATIONSHIP

Some people find this impossible. As a result, they are unable ever to get beyond the personality traits they find irritating. Result? A personality conflict often develops and the productivity of both parties and those who have to work with them is unnecessarily damaged.

Although relationships usually reflect the personalities on each side, concentrating on the relationship itself will help one ignore any irritating habits and concentrate instead on the potential benefits of successful communication with the other person. This concentration on the relationship instead of personalities also helps some people to minimise age or value differences, ethnic backgrounds or sexual orientation. Too often, these factors prevent an individual from taking a broader view. When you are able to push such matters aside and deal exclusively with the relationship itself, greater objectivity and fairness will result and things will move in a more positive direction.

It is a difficult lesson to learn but if you allow someone else's personality to irritate you into a negative attitude, you are the one who suffers. Away from work, you will want to base a personal relationship on personality, and that is to be expected. However, in the workplace, where productivity thrives on positive relationships, it can be a different matter.

Case Study 1:
Jeff and his boss

Jeff had invested almost twenty years with a growing, progressive firm. He was proud of his directorship, excellent salary, and good benefits. Recently, Jeff had allowed himself to get into a serious personality conflict with a new boss. Jeff no longer looked forward to work and his wife Sally was increasingly concerned about her husband's emotional health. As a result, she persuaded Jeff to seek professional counselling.

The counsellor suggested that Jeff could help to solve his problem by shifting the attention from the demanding personality of his boss towards the working relationship between them. Jeff got the message. Later, he and Sally decided it would help to list his boss's most irritating characteristics on a piece of paper and then burn it. They reasoned that in this way, Jeff would be able to concentrate on productivity rather than worrying about the frustrations of his boss's behaviour. Jeff said to himself: 'Why allow the odd personality of my boss to affect *my* work and career?'

What chance do you give this strategy of working?

Excellent chance ☐

No chance ☐

Worth trying. ☐

To compare your response with that of the author, turn to page 70.

Attitude and human relations

In the work environment, as in your personal life, nothing contributes more to building and maintaining healthy relationships than a positive attitude.*

What is a positive attitude?

On the surface, attitude is the way you communicate your mood to others. When you are optimistic and anticipate successful encounters, you transmit a positive attitude. Normally, your colleagues will respond favourably. When you are pessimistic and expect the worst, your attitude is often negative. When this happens, your fellow employees often avoid you or react negatively to your behaviour. Inside your head, where it all starts, attitude is a turn of the mind. It is the way you look at things, mentally.

On your way to work, think of attitude as the mental

---

* For more insight into the importance of attitude and human relations see *How to Develop a Positive Attitude* by Elwood N Chapman (Kogan Page).

outlook you have towards the day ahead. In the way that you use a camera, you can focus your mind either on positive or negative factors. You can view your workplace as an interesting environment where you can grow, learn, accomplish career goals and have some fun; or it can be a drag from the time you arrive until you leave. Perception – the complicated process of viewing and interpreting your environment – is a mental phenomenon. It is within your power to concentrate on selected aspects of your work environment and ignore others. Quite simply, you take the picture of your job and career you want to take.

Why does attitude make such a big difference?

A positive attitude will accomplish three basic goals: (1) It will boost your enthusiasm for your work and the people surrounding you; (2) It will enhance your creativity and put you in a position to increase your output, and (3) It will help you to make the most of your personality. Colleagues will find it easier to build a relationship with you and they will be motivated to keep it healthy and alive longer.

But as important as attitude may be, it is the *combination* of attitude and solid human relations skills that spell career success.

Productivity and human relations

In any team situation, each person is expected to carry a fair share of the workload. It is the responsibility of management to evaluate the individual contributions of team members. It is natural for some people to carry a slightly heavier load because of ability, experience, motivation or pride. Small productivity imbalances are no problem. But when a gap becomes notice-ably excessive, team relationships often deteriorate.

Sometimes, high producers become upset over the low pro-ductivity of others. As a result, high producers may make a fuss and lose the support of other team members or allow their own output to suffer. Result? Departmental productivity drops.

WORK ATTITUDE TEST

This exercise is designed to help you measure whether or not you are making enough effort to achieve the best possible work attitude. Circle a number from 10 down to 1. 10 indicates that you are saying you are making a supreme effort; 1 indicates that you have stopped trying to improve your attitude in this case.

	HIGH (Positive)	LOW (Negative)
1. I concentrate on adjusting my attitude each morning on the way to work	10 9 8 7 6 5 4 3 2 1	
2. If I were to guess, I think my boss would rate my attitude as a	10 9 8 7 6 5 4 3 2 1	
3. I make a serious effort each day to build positive working relationships with all my fellow-workers	10 9 8 7 6 5 4 3 2 1	
4. I believe my fellow-workers would rate my current attitude as a	10 9 8 7 6 5 4 3 2 1	
5. If a meter could gauge my sense of humour in the workplace, it would read something like	10 9 8 7 6 5 4 3 2 1	
6. I rate my enthusiasm towards my current job as a	10 9 8 7 6 5 4 3 2 1	
7. I never permit little things to influence my attitude in a negative way	10 9 8 7 6 5 4 3 2 1	
8. I would rate the attitude I communicate over the telephone as a	10 9 8 7 6 5 4 3 2 1	
9. The patience and consideration I show to others (inside or outside the organisation) deserves a rating of	10 9 8 7 6 5 4 3 2 1	
10. Based upon my work performance and general attitude, I deserve a	10 9 8 7 6 5 4 3 2 1	

TOTAL _____

A score of 90 or over is a sign that you are doing an outstanding job in terms of human relations. A score between 70 and 90 indicates that your attitude is good and you demonstrate a good understanding of human relations. A rating of between 50 and 70 suggests an improvement in your attitude would measurably improve your working relationships. If you rated yourself below 50, your human relations progress is being severely restricted by your attitude.

When John started his teaching career, his standards were so high that he allowed himself to become upset with his colleagues who had measurably lower standards. After a year in the classroom he left to take up another career. Today he looks back and realises that he would have been happier if he had remained in teaching. He freely acknowledges that he allowed the behaviour of others to put him off the career he really wanted.

For most employees, the solution to working with those who perform at lower levels is a three-step process: (1) Continue to set a good example and do your level best to ignore the personal productivity of others. (This is difficult because it may go on indefinitely.) (2) It may be possible to resolve the problem through techniques used in resolving conflicts, such as mutual understanding, bargaining or collaboration of some kind. (3) It could be necessary to take the situation to a superior in the hope that she or he is capable of resolving the imbalance. Ultimately, a solution is necessary or the high producers (those people that management wants to keep) may leave. These individuals may rightfully perceive that under such conditions, leaving is the only available option.

Relationship building with fellow-workers

Your most important working relationship is with your immediate superior. In most cases, the best way to maintain an excellent relationship with your boss is to concentrate on improving relationships with your colleagues.

Why is this so?

Perceptive supervisors look at your ability to work well with others because positive working relationships influence productivity. When superiors notice your ability to build good relationships with team members, you automatically build good relationships with them.

> When Jill started her new career with Mytech she was friendly, open and not the least bit intimidated by her superiors. Jill devoted most of her relationship-building time to her fellow-workers. Result? Her superiors were impressed by her human relations skills and the contribution she made to the team. It paid off a year later, when Jill was promoted to a supervisory role at another location.

The fact that Jill concentrated on building relationships with fellow-workers does not mean she neglected others. She did everything possible to maintain excellent relations with her immediate supervisor. She kept him informed and always made sure she provided follow-up on her projects. She was clever enough to know that any moves she made which might lead to accusations of favouritism from above could backfire. She simply let her skills at building positive relationships with others speak for her.

Communication is the life-blood of all relationships

Verbal communication between two people is the way an important relationship usually starts.

> The twenty-year relationship between Anne and Laura started when they found themselves on the same management training course. Sharing experiences at the end of each day, they built a common bond that has lasted.

Regular communication (face-to-face, telephone and written) is almost always necessary to maintain a relationship over an extended period.

> Within a year, Anne took her talents to another firm. She and Laura continued to keep up their friendship through frequent telephone calls and meeting for lunch at least once a month. The bond between them strengthened as they provided each other with mutual support and discussed plans for career moves.

Immediate, open, face-to-face communication is the best way to restore a damaged relationship.

> At one point, they had a falling out when Anne went back to Laura's company and Laura became her supervisor. Anne was not prepared for the more authoritative leadership style that Laura had developed since the old days. Laura had to hold a person-to-person meeting where the problem was openly discussed. Thanks to consideration and mutual respect on both sides, Anne and Laura became close again, despite the new manager–employee situation.

When it came to Laura and Anne, they were successful in terms of human relations because they learned to communicate, communicate, communicate! Like a delicate plant that is nurtured to maturity by means of water, fertiliser, and tender, loving care, human relationships are nurtured through communication. The next time you hear of a relationship that has fallen apart, it is safe to assume that a lack of communication played an important role in the process.

The mutual reward concept

It is usually easy to start up positive relationships in the workplace. The challenge comes in building and maintaining these relationships to the benefit of all concerned. One way to achieve this is to see that each individual receives rewards from the other party that are approximately equal in value. This simple 'reward exchange' policy is the basis for the Mutual Reward Theory.

The Mutual Reward Theory (MRT) states that for a relationship to remain healthy, both parties must benefit. That is, there has to be a voluntary, essentially equal exchange of benefits between the two parties. The rewards need not be the same in kind or number, but when one person starts to receive more than he or she gives, the relationship becomes vulnerable.

George, new to the job, and Hugh, with ten years' seniority, started out with a promising working relationship. George, a recent graduate with excellent computer skills, was always willing to leave his work station and help Hugh with specialised computer applications. In turn, Hugh willingly provided George with insights into the inner workings of the company. The relationship was mutually rewarding. Both benefited from it. If, however, either party had started to do more 'taking' than 'giving' the relationship could have begun to deteriorate.

For any relationship to remain healthy, both parties must appreciate the mutual exchange of benefits. It is therefore good human relations to make sure that the other party in any important relationship continues to receive appropriate rewards. In the situation outlined above, if George had withdrawn his computer support, a possible solution might have been for Hugh to sit down with George and work out another 'reward mix'.

The insensitivity of others can damage your relationships

The way other people treat you can cause you to react emotionally and damage an important relationship. Sometimes the other person may not realise that her or his behaviour is upsetting you. As a result, you may be harming yourself by being over-sensitive to the incident.

How often have you heard the expression, 'I can take so-and-so or leave him/her'? This usually means the person making the statement has been offended and is backing away from a relationship with that person.

To help you avoid over-reacting, put the items listed below in order of priority. Write number 1 opposite the incident that would most upset you up to a 6 for the one that would upset you the least.

I become upset when another person:

☑ Seems to ignore me at a gathering where others are present.

☑ Fails to keep what I took to be a promise.

☑ Holds back information I feel I deserve to know.

☑ Cancels an appointment.

☑ Refuses to be a good listener.

☑ Pays more attention to another person.

If a working relationship is important, do not allow it to be damaged because of situations similar to those listed above, as your career may suffer while the offending party walks away unaware of the damage he or she has caused. Most of us have allowed an important relationship to deteriorate over a minor matter that was never intended. The best way to handle situations like those mentioned is either to give the other person the benefit of the doubt, or discuss the matter openly and clear the air.

How will you react in the future?
I intend to say nothing if a situation similar to those listed occurs. I will, however, be more tolerant and give the other party the benefit of the doubt. This means I will forgive and forget quickly.   Tick here. ☐
I plan to discuss potential misinterpretations immediately to clear the air and restore the relationship as quickly as possible. Talking it over will help improve communication.   Tick here. ☐

Absenteeism and bad time-keeping damage relationships

One of the most frequent ways in which employees damage relationships with both bosses and colleagues is through unnecessary lateness and absenteeism. Here's why:

1. A poor attendance record leads to a credibility gap with superiors.

2. Frequent absence from responsibilities means a heavier workload for fellow-workers.

3. Work records that reflect heavy absenteeism and lateness are permanent and can be evaluated by other managers reviewing internal candidates for promotion.

4. In case of redundancies, cutbacks, or transfers, those with poor work records are often the first to go.

Despite the points listed above, many capable employees fail to see how they are damaging relationships all around them.

> Rebecca was, without question, the most capable technician on the team. When she was hard at work and on top of things her productivity was exceptional. But Rebecca was frequently late and periodically absent. This caused problems for other team members who had to adjust their workloads to offset Rebecca's lack of reliability.
>
> Ultimately, Rebecca's career was permanently damaged because of persistent absenteeism. When asked about it, she replied: 'I took a chance and lost. I didn't have to be late or absent, I just thought that I was good enough to get away with it. When my colleagues got tired of bailing me out, the game was up.'

For some strange reason, many otherwise clever people fail to see the human relations aspects of being late or absent. By refusing to discipline themselves, their credibility is in question even when they have legitimate reasons for being late or even away from work.

Case Study 2
Jennifer's image

Jennifer, an experienced professional office worker, was immediately impressed with Vicky when she joined the

RELATIONSHIP REWARD – CONFLICT CHART

One way to create conflict within a relationship is failure to behave in the manner expected by the other person. The column on the left lists some of the actions/rewards that help to *maintain* a relationship. The column on the right demonstrates that when the same rewards are *not* provided they become 'conflict points'. Feel free to add your own.

REWARDS	CONFLICT POINTS
Free and open communication	Unwilling or poor communication
Accepting differences in priority	Prejudice
Carrying full responsibility	Failure to pull expected weight
Balance of rewards	Unequal reward system
Trust	Lack of trust
Recognising the independence of others	Jealousy
Sense of humour	Lack of humour
Sensitive to needs	Insensitive to needs
Generous (with time, talent, money, etc)	Excessively mean
Keeping others informed	Failure to inform
Plenty of patience	Little patience
Keeps promises	Forgets promises
Seldom absent	Frequently absent
Excellent follow-up	Little follow-up
In control of own personal problems	Burdens colleagues with problems
Remains forward-looking	Consistently negative
_____	_____
_____	_____

Those who provide colleagues (and friends) with a good and consistent 'reward mix' will maintain excellent relationships. Those who fail to do so create conflict points that damage relationships.

department. Jennifer went out of her way to help Vicky to feel comfortable in her new environment. As a result, Vicky introduced Jennifer socially to friends out of working hours. Soon they were enjoying evenings out together and ended up sharing a flat. On the surface, it seemed to be a mutually rewarding arrangement. But after a few months, it became apparent that Vicky did not have a genuine interest in her job. She never got to grips with it and her colleagues had to help with her workload.

Soon, to everyone's surprise, Jennifer started making excuses for her friend. Although Jennifer had an excellent image and was considered management material before Vicky arrived, she was now regarded as someone with questionable judgement. Without being fully aware of what was happening, Jennifer became a victim in what had started out as a legitimate mutually-rewarding relationship. Looking back later, Jennifer made these comments:

'I made a serious human relations mistake. My need to be more socially accepted and have a good time blinded me. In time, it became obvious that Vicky was hanging on to my coat-tails at work and I was hanging on to hers for my social life. Things got out of balance when she used my personal productivity and status to keep her job. When it got so bad that Vicky was dismissed, I had to rebuild my image with colleagues and management. It won't happen again.'

Would it have been possible for Jennifer to maintain her professional status and still keep an outside relationship with Vicky? Why did it take Jennifer so long to realise what was happening? See the author's response on page 70.

When your career seems on hold

In the path of each career there are periods when an individual must stand still as far as upward mobility is concerned. There may be promotions in the future, but for the time being the organisation can do nothing for you. This is known as a 'plateau period'.

Such a period needs to be understood, because it can have a negative effect on a person, which can cause the individual to neglect his or her opportunities to improve human relations.

> Due to slower than expected growth and some restructuring, management was aware that it would be a difficult waiting period for Colin and Mark. Both were advised to be patient and continue to look forward to promotions which should eventually materialise. Mark accepted this and used the waiting period to improve relationships and hone his skills. Colin, on the other hand, became discouraged and let things slip. When the state of affairs improved, Mark was promoted, but Colin was not ready. Talking it over with the personnel manager, Colin was told: 'When you failed to maintain a positive attitude, stay involved and carry on working hard, you disqualified yourself.'

Plateau periods are never easy. It is difficult to keep learning and stay positive when you feel you are ready for more responsibility but nothing happens. Occasionally you might have to put Plan B into action (see page 62). But for those who want to remain with an organisation and make progress, staying interested and involved is essential in order to avoid career damage.

Turning a family problem into a career advantage

Jack Smith, a highly regarded columnist for a major newspaper, is quoted as having said: 'A person must try to worry about things that aren't important so he won't worry about things that are.' The suggestion is a good one, especially when it comes to worrying about major changes at home while your career falls apart.

Whoever you are, you have probably experienced some worries in your home or family life. When you permit these legitimate concerns to spill over into your work performance, your career often suffers.

How does one keep family problems out of the workplace?

It may sound confusing and contradictory, but having a problem outside the workplace can often be a career advantage. This happens when the employee learns to escape the personal dilemma temporarily by devoting more effort to his or her job.

> When Simon's marriage fell apart, he felt terrible. To keep things together, he threw himself into his work. He told himself: 'If I let my personal life damage my career, I will be a victim twice over. I refuse to let this happen.'

> Once Sheri knew her ex-husband had run off and left her with two children to bring up, she buried herself in her job. It helped her not to dwell on negatives and improved her role as a provider. She told herself: 'I'll show everybody I can survive as a single parent.'

> Mrs Smith, a corporate executive in her fifties, was being driven to distraction by her thirty-year-old son who was constantly in trouble. Rather than drive her friends away by talking about it, she devoted most of her efforts to her career. She said: 'I can't control my son's life, but I can enhance my own through a good career.'

Three common misunderstandings

Sometimes, without being aware of it, we fall into situations that needlessly turn people against us. Have any of the following happened to you?

1. Failure to give others a second chance

It is true that we do not always get a second chance to make a good first impression on others. But we may lose more than we suspect when we refuse to give people a second chance to build a relationship with *us*.

> When Brenda first met Cynthia (both were new managers brought in from outside) she decided not to pursue a relationship with the other girl as Cynthia mishandled their first encounter. In other words, Brenda did not give Cynthia a second chance. A year later, when Cynthia became Brenda's boss, Brenda realised she had damaged her career, unnecessarily.

2. Expecting management to provide motivation

When we hold management responsible for providing us with the productivity incentives that will keep us motivated, we usually miss the boat and wonder what went wrong.

> Within two months of getting a job, Paul decided that no one cared about his work and his attitude became negative. His productivity dropped below the level it was when he first started. This led to a special meeting with his supervisor. She stated that the company was providing the best possible working environment and Paul was responsible for his attitude and motivation. Paul took exception to her advice and resigned. When his next job (which took him six months to get) provided a working environment less attractive than the one he had left, Paul began to understand that attitude and motivation are 'do-it-yourself' projects wherever you are.

3. Releasing frustrations

Psychologists tell us it is healthy to let off a little steam now and then. But when this is done in front of colleagues, relationships can be damaged.

> Stella became so frustrated with her boss two weeks ago that she stormed out of the office and didn't return until the following day. Although Stella and her boss patched things up, there was little she could do to restore relationships with colleagues who had witnessed the incident. Stella had to learn the hard way to release her frustrations in a harmless manner away from work.

Summary

☐ Many employees, including managers, underestimate the importance of building strong human relations. These individuals do not bother to learn good human relations skills and consequently their career progress is slowed down.

☐ Human relations skills (of which there are many) are perhaps more important to career success than technical skills.

☐ A positive attitude plays a key role in the success of human relationships.

☐ Good communication is the life-blood of all strong relationships.

☐ One way to avoid harming a relationship is to not be too sensitive to minor personality differences.

☐ Using the Mutual Reward Theory will help to build, maintain, and/or repair important relationships.

☐ Most employees who are consistently late for work or frequently absent damage relationships with others who have to do their work for them.

☐ There is a direct correlation between how team members relate to each other and the resulting productivity.

☐ Maintaining good human relations during career plateau periods is critical to one's ability to make progress at work.

☐ Employees who are good at human relations make an honest attempt to repair damaged relationships as soon as possible. They do this even when the other party is mostly to blame.

CHAPTER 2

Repairing Human Relationships

The willingness factor

Like abandoned cars, many relationships are left on the side of the road to rust. Even when repairing a relationship is important to an individual's career, no real effort is made to patch things up. Many individuals choose to walk away from a promising situation rather than restore a damaged relationship. It is sometimes difficult to understand why.

One reason may be because one party is reluctant or unwilling to discuss the matter. The only way to act over this is to start a conversation with that person. A fairly painless way of doing this could be to make a frank statement such as, 'I'm a bit worried about the state of relations between us. How do you think we can improve things?' Of course, everyone must use an approach that he or she finds acceptable.

The following tips may help you to initiate a discussion along these lines:

- Find something amusing to share.
- Become a better listener.
- Be willing to give a little more than you get.
- Let the other person save face.

The mending of any relationship rests on a desire by both parties to try. If there is a genuine willingness on your part, you may discover the same attitude in the other person. Simply making the effort to talk about how to patch things up could turn you into a human relations winner.

What have you really got to lose?

RELATIONSHIP REPAIR ASSESSMENT EXERCISE

Most relationship conflicts can be resolved. A few cannot. Individuals are often so ambivalent about trying to restore a relationship that they back away without making an effort. The purpose of the following exercise is to prevent you from doing this. If you come up with 'yes' answers to many of the questions below you should make a supreme effort to repair any damage, no matter who caused it in the first place. You will get the best results if you think about a genuine relationship conflict you are facing. Answer all questions.

Your relationship conflict – ask yourself: Yes   No

1. Is the relationship important to your future? ☐ ☐

2. Has the relationship been rewarding in the past? ☐ ☐

3. Are you really willing to communicate openly about the conflict? ☐ ☐

4. Are you willing to sit down and discuss possible solutions with the other person? ☐ ☐

5. Would you consider arranging a meeting with the other person regardless of how the conflict started? ☐ ☐

6. If attempts at resolving the conflict fail, will you consider yourself the main victim? ☐ ☐

7. If restoration fails, will others also become victims? ☐ ☐

8. Do you honestly want the other person to feel that the relationship has been repaired? ☐ ☐

9. Can you ignore irritating personality traits in order to repair the relationship? ☐ ☐

10. Can you forgive and forget? ☐ ☐

Number of 'Yes' answers ☐

If you answered YES to eight or more questions, the possibilities of repairing the relationship are excellent. You should not hesitate to arrange a meeting. Four or more YES answers indicate that possibilities of restoration are very good. Three or fewer YES answers is a sign that attempts at reparation may be unlikely to produce results.

Open communication

If good communication is the life-blood of any healthy relationship, then a transfusion of free, open communication should be the first order of business in any repair to a relationship. It is important to pick the right time (when you think the other person will be receptive), the right place (private and free from interruptions), and to see that the discussion opens in a quiet, non-threatening manner.

Once the time and place are right and both parties are comfortable, you should state in your own way that you would like to discuss how to restore the relationship and keep it healthy. You should ask the other party to tell you what it will take to adjust the system so that both of you will benefit in the future.

It took Jean three days to get up her nerve and pick the right time to start a discussion with Harry over their recent falling out. Although she felt awkward while getting the conversation going and introducing her interpretation of a winners-all theory, Harry quickly picked up the idea and within 20 minutes they had worked out a new 'reward' system that formed the basis of a new and better working relationship.

Mutual Reward Theory (or winners-all) is only one approach that can be used to restore a relationship. You may wish to find another that you feel more comfortable with.

Resolving conflicts

Robert B Maddux in his book *Team Building: An Exercise in Leadership* points out that there are many types of conflict resolution, as illustrated overleaf.

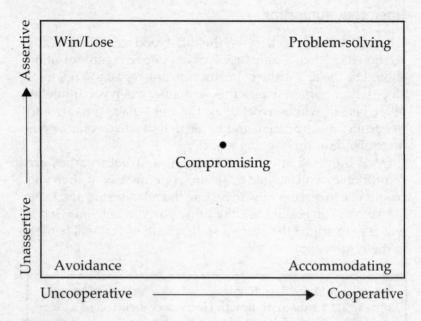

Interpreting the above chart indicates that if someone is unassertive and uncooperative the style is *avoidance*; if someone is unassertive and cooperative that person is *accommodating*; if the person is assertive and uncooperative she or he is playing a *win/lose* game. Obviously, someone who is assertive, cooperative and compromising is more likely to resolve conflicts. Even when differences exist, the key is willingness to compromise.

Compromise or be victimised?

In most one-to-one human situations, some compromise is necessary if the relationship is to be maintained. Often a little give from one side will do the trick. Generally, both parties must relax their position from time to time.

Why is compromise often so difficult?

One reason may be because many people establish such rigid and defiant positions to begin with that any compromise could be interpreted as weakness or failure.

> Peter took such a firm stand with his boss over not accepting a temporary assignment that he would not allow himself to compromise. Later, he discovered his stand had caused a serious upset and he had second thoughts about compromising, but it was too late.

From an MRT perspective, a compromise often simply means shifting some of the benefits or rewards. Rather than 'giving in' and perhaps losing face, one party may agree to provide a different reward than the one anticipated in exchange for a substitute better than the one currently being received.

> Under the company's flexitime arrangements, Jill wanted to start work at 9:00 am instead of 8:00 am so that she could drop her daughter off at school. The only one in the department Jill could find to cover for her was Sandra who was single. When Jill approached Sandra, she was unhappy about making the change until the boss explained that the earlier starting time would give Sandra an opportunity to operate a new machine that would improve her skills. Sandra quickly compromised and accepted the new work schedule.

When there is a dispute between two people, a substitution of rewards can sometimes create two winners.

Restoring a damaged relationship with a superior

Your most important working relationship is with your immediate superior. If something damages this sensitive relationship (no matter who is to blame) immediate repair work is recommended.

How do you go about this?

The first thing to remember is that you must not allow a small injury to become a major one. Think through the issue. Just how are you being affected? Tell your point of view to a friend who can see the problem more objectively.

Second, pick the right time to approach your superior. She

or he may be too busy (or concerned with other problems) on a particular day to talk to you. If so, wait a bit longer. Pick a time (and place) when you can talk freely and your boss has time to discuss things.

Remember that not all superiors are comfortable with their roles. In fact most people are not well trained in resolving conflict. They may genuinely want to be considerate and fair but lack of experience, technique or pressures can interfere. Do not expect perfection. Be satisfied with the best repair job that you can manage under the circumstances.

Bear in mind that you should be more interested in repairing the relationship than bringing about any changes in your boss's behaviour which would suit you better. Your boss is entitled to his or her personality, just as you are entitled to yours.

When rebuilding a relationship with a superior, the following suggestions will help you to make a good job of it. You should:

- Keep up your personal productivity.
- Maintain good relationships with your colleagues.
- Let it be known through your attitude that you value your work.
- Refuse to say anything against your supervisor in front of others.

If you allow a superior to intimidate you, a healthy, two-way relationship will be impossible. The chances are that this will not be the case because most managers know that they are assessed on the performance of their staff.

Case Study 3
Relationship reversal

Three years ago Mr Johnson was promoted to the position of office manager in a large financial institution. He quickly discovered that his new boss had trouble in communicating. She was abrupt and didn't seem at all interested in Mr Johnson's career.

When discussing his boss's communication problems with his wife, she suggested he should arrange to have a discussion with her on how they could best work together. At the first opportunity, Mr Johnson asked his boss what he could contribute in his new post. The next day, Mr Johnson made a summary of his boss's expectations and wrote out a list of work-oriented goals based on her ideas. Mr Johnson asked his boss to comment on them. Slowly, by fulfilling some of his boss's expectations, the things *he* wanted (such as more open communication) began to be forthcoming. Eventually a solid relationship emerged, and Mr Johnson was recently named as a replacement to his boss who was also promoted.

In using the MRT approach, did Mr Johnson forestall a conflict that might have turned him into a victim? To compare your answer with that of the author, turn to page 70.

Dealing with sharks

Near every shoal of saltwater fish, you find a few sharks (or other predators). In every work environment, you are likely to find a similarly aggressive (sometimes unscrupulous) employee. These individuals can be so devious and insensitive that they are not worried about making you (or anyone else) a victim.

How do you deal with these sharks?

First and foremost, it is vital to understand that predators usually thrive on passive souls. At first, they may appear hostile to those who stand up to them (harsh reactions are typical), but they often silently respect (or fear) competitors. So the first thing to do is to let a shark know that he or she will have trouble turning you into a victim. When pushed, you too can be tough.

Victoria used every trick in the book to undermine Patsy in order to get the new job colleagues knew Patsy had earned. Finally, Patsy invited Victoria for coffee and said: 'Victoria, my career is as important to me as yours is to you. I don't mind competition, but I want you to know that I do not intend to move over for you. Don't let my name Patsy fool you. I'm not weak. Do you understand?'

In building relationships with sharks, you should always bear the following in mind:

- Do not expect your superior or fellow-workers to protect you.
- An improved relationship can often be built after a confrontation.
- If you find you have an emotional reaction after standing up to a colleague, seek the support of people outside work to help alleviate the side effects.

Case Study 4
William and Philip

Both William and Philip started their careers in a large organisation at the same time. It soon became obvious, however, that their philosophy towards work was radically different.

A quiet, introspective person, William does his best to maintain peaceful, easy-going relationships with everyone. Philip is more competitive. He enjoys confrontations. Philip has learned that if he can upset another person emotionally, he often comes out ahead. He has the ability to handle heated situations better than others. Philip does not feel guilty when it comes to using this technique. So far his strategy seems to be working: although younger than William, he occupies a more responsible position.

How would you advise people like William to deal with those like Philip? To compare your answers with those of the author turn to page 71.

Summary

☐ The first step in repairing a relationship is a willingness to communicate.

☐ The MRT approach to resolving a conflict may be your best bet.

☐ Some degree of compromise is usually required from each party when resolving a conflict.

☐ It often takes all the methods at your disposal to restore a relationship with a supervisor.

☐ Sharks are less likely to attack fellow-workers who stand up to them.

CHAPTER 3
The Self-Victimising Process

Understanding the self-victimisation process

It often happens that a conflict will emerge within a relationship and both parties become increasingly involved in an emotional/psychological process that can reach higher and more damaging stages. Three levels of damage are:

Stage 1: Surface damage with low risk of serious repercussions. Restoration possibilities are excellent if action is taken immediately by either party. No permanent harm need result.

Stage 2: Deeper damage to relationship. Emotional harm may be more serious to one individual than the other. Restoration becomes more difficult. One person may well be on the way to becoming a victim.

Stage 3: Emotional/psychological conflict severe. Both parties are likely to be victims. Restoration often depends upon the willingness of both to communicate openly. Professional help may be needed.

The process will vary depending on the individual and the nature of the conflict. But the point is that once started, it is often a continuous development until one or both parties become losers. Even if one person removes him or herself from the situation (ie opts out), 'self-victimisation' can continue.

The sooner any damage, no matter how slight, is repaired

the better. Just as both individuals can lose, if proper timely action is taken, both can also win.

The price is high

People who are unfortunate enough to be the victims either of unintentional accidents or deliberate crimes, often pay a terrible price. The consequences can be similarly serious if and when we become human relations victims. In extreme cases, it can affect our whole career progress. Consider the following:

- Statistically, only a small percentage of people become victims of a serious crime. Everyone eventually becomes the victim of a damaged relationship.

- Financial loss due to theft, fraud or physical injury can be high. So can the loss of a career opportunity.

- The emotional and psychological damage suffered by a human relations victim can sometimes be as traumatic as that of the victim of a crime.

Human conflicts can tear people apart emotionally. They may be so badly affected that their productivity drops. It is not unusual for people to adopt a negative attitude and lose sight of work goals. The victim of a damaged relationship can experience moodiness, loss of confidence, resentment, indignation, mental distress and in extreme cases, may resort to violence.

More employees resign because of a relationship conflict than for any other reason. Has it ever happened to you?

Impact on career progress

In almost any human relations conflict you either end up as a winner (by resolving the situation) or a loser (by becoming a victim).

Last week Hazel and Janet had an argument over a minor matter to do with work schedules. Emotions ran high. Janet got over it within the hour, but Hazel took the incident personally and sulked around the office for the rest of the week. Her work suffered and her supervisor noticed an unusually negative attitude towards colleagues and customers alike. From a human relations point of view, Janet had outsmarted Hazel by refusing to become a victim over a trivial matter.

When a conflict arises, you should aim to repair the relationship as soon as possible without hurting yourself or the other party. It is difficult to make progress in your career if you leave a trail of damaged relationships behind you. You should also be aware of the psychological damage you are capable of doing to yourself. Human relations mistakes (and no one is immune) are damaging enough when the issues are resolved quickly. But when we turn the conflict inwards and become victims ourselves, the damage is made far worse.

Victimisation can occur in many ways. Sometimes it comes from being over-sensitive to small matters (minor rebuffs, unintentional slights, etc). At other times, major problems such as deep-seated personality conflicts (eg prejudice) can cause severe damage to our self-esteem. There are also times when we allow conflicts away from work to spill over into the workplace and harm our careers. All of us, at some time or other, have to deal with fragile, awkward, human relations situations. When we can handle these without becoming victims ourselves, we benefit. By learning how to deal with people of every kind, we show that we are successful at human relations and become true winners.

AWARENESS EXERCISE

This exercise is designed to help you become more aware of how everyday situations can turn you into a victim unnecessarily. First, study each situation. Next, sort the list into order of priority by placing a 1 in the box opposite the statement that is most likely to turn you into a victim, a 2 opposite the next most likely situation and so on. Please add any tricky situations of your own at the bottom.

☐ Embarrassing yourself by becoming upset in public over slow service.

☐ Going over and over a minor human relations mistake in your mind until you begin to lose sleep over it.

☐ Refusing to apologise over a small human relations mistake.

☐ Holding a grudge because of a simple mistake made by another person.

☐ Refusing to let another person apologise for hurting your feelings.

☐ Becoming furious over a bill that seems too large, or was sent in error.

☐ Paying too much attention to one colleague and putting good relationships with other team members at risk.

☐ Getting frustrated with a computer or other machine because it will not work properly for you.

☐ Becoming frustrated trying to fight bureaucratic red tape.

☐ Allowing someone who doesn't perform to your expectations to raise your blood pressure.

OTHER SITUATIONS:

☐ _____

☐ _____

☐ _____

Three ways in which people victimise themselves

1. When they refuse to correct mistakes quickly

Jack knew he had upset Ralph when he didn't include him in a decision-making meeting. He quickly apologised, said how much he valued their relationship and invited him to lunch. Before lunch was over the relationship had been fully restored.

2. When they allow a 'no fault' situation to go unchecked

It became obvious to everyone but Pat that the misunderstanding was nobody's fault and a classic, almost laughable case of bad communication. Even so, Robert – the only one who could be deeply hurt by the situation – played it safe and took Pat out to dinner to discuss what had happened and satisfy himself that their relationship was back on a sound footing. When asked by a colleague why he had taken the initiative Robert replied: 'Nobody was to blame but I didn't want to run the risk of becoming a victim just because Pat didn't see the overall picture.'

3. When they allow the emotional side of a conflict to grind away at them

When John and Mr Andrew had a dispute, John's feelings turned inwards to the point that he couldn't sleep at night. Soon his work began to suffer. Mr Andrew, with more experience and objectivity, was able to cope with the emotional side more easily. Result? John remained so disturbed by the incident that he resigned – even though he liked his job. John became the primary victim.

EXERCISE: WHO WILL BECOME THE VICTIM?

The temptation to blame other people for normal human problems is natural. However, we can become victims even when others are at fault. Listed below are some typical work-place problems. As you read them, ask yourself: 'Who will be the ultimate victim?'

1. You let off steam about an irritating habit of your boss's and the word gets back to him.

2. One colleague is a 'know-all' and you let it get under your skin.

3. You and your boss have a fundamental misunderstanding in communication over deadlines.

4. A careless fellow-worker forgets to tell you about an important telephone call from a customer and you lose the account.

5. While under pressure your boss takes it out on you in front of the office staff but apologises in private the next day.

6. To your bitter disappointment your request to go to a meeting in another town is turned down.

7. You discover that your boss has adopted an idea you discussed with a colleague a few weeks ago and has given that person the credit.

8. You discover that a fellow employee has told on you for unintentionally violating a safety rule.

Your reactions to the above situations could turn you into a victim. It is a difficult lesson to learn, but as far as being a victim is concerned, it doesn't always matter who is at fault. When faced with similar situations in the future, why not give your-self prior warning by asking the following question?

Am I becoming a victim?

High-risk working relationships

Generally speaking, the more important a relationship is, the higher the risk of someone being badly hurt when a conflict arises. This is the 'high involvement high vulnerability' principle. It states that the more involved and intense a relationship becomes, the more vulnerable you are when things go wrong. Three critical factors are involved in all working relationships.

1. Frequency of contact

If you fall out with someone you work with on a daily basis, you are more likely to become a victim than if the disagreement is with a more distant colleague. Daily contact can intensify a conflict even though there is plenty of opportunity for communication (and resolving the disagreement).

2. Nature of relationship

Your relationship with your superior is far more complex than with most of your colleagues. Such factors as authority, performance, assessment and discipline are involved. Maintaining a relationship with a superior often takes more attention, care, and perception.

3. Personal involvement

The better you know a colleague socially, the more sensitive the issue can become if a dispute arises. This is the reason why many experienced workers choose to keep their personal and working relationships separate.

Some working relationships require more effort to maintain them than others. In most cases, the people you are most involved with are the ones who will come to your aid when you need it. But they can also damage you the most in times of conflict.

Have you ever experienced the high involvement high vulnerability principle?

Your colleagues may seem sympathetic when you are

involved in a dispute with someone at work while at the same time secretly wondering why you are so intent on turning yourself into a victim.

A victim-prone relationship

Outside marriage, no arrangement makes more demands on the Mutual Reward Theory than a 50/50 business partnership. This is because the legal structure of a partnership is designed to establish an equal reward system that is virtually impossible to maintain. Each partner is supposed to contribute equal energy, talent, hours and capital to the success of the venture. When one partner considers that the other is not contributing as much as the other, a conflict can result.

Liz and Carol decided to open a day-care centre on a 50/50 partnership basis. They spent a great many hours researching and planning the operation, but neither took the time to look closely at the *kind* of relationship they hoped to establish. Were they compatible? Did they understand the division of duties? Could they make it work? After both families had contributed their savings (and taken out second mortgages), the operation was launched with great success. The profit at the end of the first year was greater than either Liz or Carol had hoped to achieve. Even so, the business eventually failed. Neither Liz nor Carol could maintain an acceptable working relationship because neither could agree on the level of contribution the other was making to the business.

Few relationships are as demanding as a business partnership, but *all* relationships contain a stress factor. When the stress falls more heavily on one person than the other, that individual is vulnerable and may become the primary victim. Although Liz and Carol became financial victims because their business failed, the emotional damage was more serious because it broke up a 20-year friendship.

Case Study 5
The vulnerable professor

Dr Franklin was highly regarded by his colleagues at Uptown University. He was treated with sensitivity and given every consideration. When he decided to expand his department, he was given immediate authority to advertise for and take on an assistant.

After several interviews, he selected a much younger, but highly qualified candidate. In the first year, they appeared to have a solid working relationship. Then philosophical differences arose and the students began to divide themselves into the camp of either Dr Franklin or his assistant. Soon, the two started to avoid each other. Then they stopped communicating completely. Without communication, the situation got worse. Four years later, Dr Franklin took early retirement to avoid any further emotional distress. To those aware of what was going on, it was obvious that Dr Franklin had become the primary victim.

What might Dr Franklin have done in the early stages to avoid the conflict arising in the first place? What corrective steps might he have taken to restore the relationship? Is it a fair statement to say that Dr Franklin victimised himself? Compare your answers with those of the author on page 71.

Knowing your vulnerability

Sometimes it is important to defend a principle even though it is controversial and will cause an upset. An important consideration in taking such a stand is whether or not you will victimise yourself.

For many reasons (personality, type of upbringing, cultural background, etc) some people are more easily able to cope with emotions that accompany conflict. Others will suppress their feelings and allow the conflict to seriously disrupt their lives.

> Rachel and Janice would go into a management meeting with the same amount of enthusiasm. If the meeting was non-controversial, they would leave feeling the same way as when they arrived. However, if emotions ran high, Rachel could put it behind her before leaving work while Janice would lose sleep and did not get over the effect of the controversy for several days.

People who cannot prevent relationship conflicts from upsetting them are more vulnerable to self-victimisation than those who have the ability to take a step back. As a result, they must learn to play their cards differently. This may mean taking a closer look at the principle to see if it is worth defending, or perhaps preparing themselves better in order to remain more objective, or in some cases finding an acceptable compromise or substitute.

If you want to become a martyr, make sure the issue merits it. Only when your values have been severely violated should you leave a job. If it is a difference of opinion, you must remember that you could be wrong. Study the opposing view with an open mind to make sure of your position. If you are wrong, the outcome could be a positive learning experience instead of a major career change.

Becoming a martyr in most business environments is a good way to damage your career progress permanently.

Why are people blind to self-victimisation?

When people realise that they have become involved in a relationship conflict, few have the insight or experience to back away and look at the overall picture before making an effort to patch things up. Once an individual learns how to do this, he or she might approach the same situation differently, with much better results.

> Steve was so upset over the relationship with his new boss that he almost resigned on the spot. Keeping his emotions under control, he and a friend sat down to look at the conflict in detail. When Steve and his friend assessed the situation from every angle (Steve's seniority, experience, work contacts, image, etc), it became clear that Steve would become a needless victim if his boss came out on top. It was hard on Steve's ego but he decided to compromise and work to rebuild the relationship. Today Steve is a senior manager in the organisation and his former superior no longer works there.

Three basic factors make it difficult to see the forest (your career) for the trees (your current emotional stress.) They are:

1. The 'eye for an eye' syndrome

When an employee is under stress from a relationship conflict, it is natural to blame the other person.

> When the sales manager gave a choice sales territory to Jane, Frank exploded. He laid the blame at the sales manager's door. His hostility cost him the opportunity of being considered for the position of assistant sales manager (a better opportunity than staying in the field) which was to be reviewed in a few weeks. As a result of the turmoil, Frank resigned in order to save face. Looking back, Frank knows he victimised himself and threw away a good career opportunity with a quality company.

2. Accepting advice from the wrong sources

When you get into a dispute, it is possible to gain a better perspective by talking things over with another person. *But not always.* The wrong person can pour fuel on the fire and the situation can get worse, with both parties ending up further away from a solution.

> Claire was so upset when the promotion was given to Jeremy that she needed to talk to someone. She chose Geraldine and Mary. Neither of them knew all of the facts, and they persuaded Claire to file a sex discrimination charge. The preliminary investigation showed that Jeremy was more highly qualified and that management had made a sound decision. By the time Claire backed away from the investigation, her relationship with Geraldine and Mary was over, Claire realised she had victimised herself unnecessarily because of poor advice from two fellow-workers.

Talking the issue over with an objective observer (Geraldine and Mary were not objective) can ease some of the pain and put the issue into perspective. A few possibilities might be: (1) someone in the personnel department; (2) a trusted adviser; (3) a senior colleague whom you can take into your confidence.

3. Letting your ego stand in the way

When it comes to relationships, everyone makes mistakes. Frequently, those with experience and high in self-esteem make the simple mistakes in judgement that one might expect from an inexperienced employee. When this happens, the ego of the more experienced employee can stand in the way of a solution in which there are no victims.

> Mr Judson found it humiliating when the quarterly report showed that Ms Kay, a new manager of a branch operation similar to his, had beaten his previous quarterly sales record. The next time he and Ms Kay met, Mr Judson made some demeaning comments and a disagreement flared up that became common knowledge throughout the firm. In the months that followed Mr Judson tried so hard to beat Ms Kay that he neglected other responsibilities. Eventually the managing director was forced to have a word with him. Result? Ms Kay got a promotion that Mr Judson could have had had his ego not got in the way.

In the area of human relationships, it is all too possible to win a battle but lose the war. An individual can become so involved in the psychology of conflict that he or she fails to recognise the self-destruction that is taking place.

Case Study 6
Disposable relationships

In all her 32 years Denise had never felt more of a victim. Her career path had been halted because of staff cuts in the company, a trusted colleague had told tales on her, and she was extremely upset by the acrimony of her divorce proceedings which had been going on for several weeks.

Talking to her sister, Helen, she commented: 'I've decided never to have a serious relationship again. That way, when they don't work out I can scrap them. Serious relationships in all areas of my life have a habit of kicking me in the face.'

Helen replied: 'I don't agree. We all need deep relationships, both at work and in our personal lives. It's quality that counts, not quantity. I think you should keep an open mind and enjoy being with people. But you also have to grow up and find a way of developing and maintaining *good* relationships. It's not the number of flowers in your garden, it's the beauty of the ones you have. Your problem is that every time a relationship goes bad, you feel sorry for yourself and become more of a loner. If you don't learn to build and take care of rewarding relationships, you will continue to be a victim. You are going to turn into a recluse.'

What flaws, if any, do you find in Helen's argument? Is she guilty of being simplistic in her approach? Compare your thoughts with those of the author on page 71.

Summary

☐ Only a few of us become the victims of serious crimes, but eventually all of us become human relations victims.

☐ The victimisation process tends to speed up unless immediate steps are taken to resolve conflict.

- [ ] You can become the primary victim even if you are not to blame.

- [ ] Self-victimisation occurs when you cannot handle the emotional strain that goes with a relationship conflict.

- [ ] Most people are so involved in the emotional side of a conflict that they are not aware of how they are victimising themselves.

CHAPTER 4
Preparing a Winning Strategy

Putting it all together

A quick review

Chapter 1 demonstrated that by following certain principles, you could build and maintain better relationships with superiors and fellow-workers.

Chapter 2 gave you a tried and tested approach to use in repairing damaged relationships.

Chapter 3 explained the self-victimisation process to teach you how to do a better job of protecting yourself in future human conflicts.

The challenge

Chapter 4 will provide you with an opportunity to create a master plan from what you have learned. This chapter outlines practical techniques that will help you to build and maintain quality relationships effectively. If you can achieve this you will enhance your career progress and earn the compliment of being considered successful at human relations.

Ten techniques or practical tips follow. Based on your experience, insight and personal way of doing things, you are invited to challenge each. Please state at the end of each technique whether you agree, disagree, or are uncertain by putting a tick in the appropriate box. Then review your answers and work to incorporate those with which you agree into your human relations plan for the future.

Technique 1
Create and maintain a variety of relationships

In any job, there are many relationships to be created and maintained. In addition to superiors and fellow-workers, there are usually clients and key people in other departments who are important to your career progress. A secretary, security guard, or maintenance man should not be ignored.

Colleagues, however, deserve special attention for the following reasons:

1. When you help colleagues to produce more, you enhance your own reputation.

> Although Mike's output was average, management recognised that he was always helping team members with technical problems and contributed to their higher productivity.

2. When you have a good attendance record and arrive on time each day you make things easier for your supervisor and fellow-workers.

> Although Alice was slower than others in serving customers, she was never late and seldom absent. Whenever another department member didn't show up, Alice took on the extra work without complaint.

3. When colleagues like you they can influence management to promote you.

> Martin, through his positive attitude, earned the respect of colleagues as well as superiors. When the role of manager came up, three colleagues told management they could work well with Martin.

Other relationships should not be neglected. But for those who want to impress management that they are adept at human relations, an excellent place to demonstrate such skills is with fellow-workers.

AGREE   **DISAGREE**   **UNCERTAIN**

☐   ☐   ☐

Technique 2
See relationships – not personalities

You will be taking a major step in improving relationships and avoiding conflicts when you learn to concentrate on the relationship, *not* the personality of the other person. Easy enough to say, but sometimes hard to accomplish!

> Mrs Miller had high standards of dress and manners. She could find little right with her colleague Mr Clarke. Without realising the negative implications, she often criticised him in public by commenting on his lack of polish. When her superior suggested she look at the contribution Mr Clarke was making to the department and not at his habits of dress or imperfect grammar, her attitude started to change. Although Mrs Miller would not choose to mix socially with Mr Clarke, she recognised that he was a career professional with many talents.

To keep working relationships in good order, it is best to look at what people do rather than how they appear on the surface. Work habits are what is important on the job not minor personality quirks. Do your colleagues do their best to carry a full workload? Do they cooperate and work well with others? Are they willing to learn? Do they have special talents that contribute to team productivity?

Professional employees should concentrate on working relationships and attempt to stay away from a critical analysis of personalities. Those who go in for character assassination create human conflicts and can easily end up as victims.

AGREE   **DISAGREE**   **UNCERTAIN**

☐   ☐   ☐

Technique 3
Practise the Mutual Reward Theory

When it comes to a one-to-one session with someone with whom you have a disagreement, a direct approach is not always the best. For many people a confrontation may be too stressful and uncomfortable. Answer? A better plan may be to start a discussion that develops a *mutual reward* approach.

The Mutual Reward Theory states that for a human relationship to remain healthy over an extended period the benefits should be fairly equally divided between both parties. What is important is that each participant regards what they receive from the relationship as satisfactory to him or her. Both individuals should feel they come out on top. The idea is to introduce the other person to the mutual reward concept.

> Ian, sensing that his working relationship with Freda was deteriorating, set up a meeting in her office and said: 'Freda, until now we have worked well together. But I get the feeling we are beginning to work against each other instead of pulling together. I would like your ideas on how we can carry on a satisfactory working relationship.'

Using the mutual reward idea is a good one because it adopts an oblique rather than a confrontational approach. Not only is it easier to use, but with open communication a more satisfactory 'reward mix' usually develops. In almost all relationship conflicts, reconciliation depends upon the creation of a more satisfactory reward system. This is the true meaning of 'give and take' or 'compromise' in conflict resolution.

AGREE	DISAGREE	UNCERTAIN
☐	☐	☐

Technique 4
Dismiss minor irritations

Years ago my wife and I were waiting for an employee to bring our car to the front of a restaurant where we had enjoyed a delightful dinner. When the car arrived I noticed a large dent in the rear bumper and immediately lost my temper. After embarrassing both my wife and myself, we discovered the employee had brought another customer's car that was identical to ours. Our car was undamaged. I didn't sleep well that night, but it was my own fault. I had shot off the handle before assessing the situation properly. I had victimised myself.

How many times have you seen anyone come away the winner when making a fuss over slow service in a restaurant or complaining to a post office employee? Did anyone really do themselves any good by telling somebody off on the telephone or getting angry in a traffic jam? Or, worst of all, exploding at work?

You might think it is good to let off steam, but in most cases like the one above, a person with a short fuse either damages his or her image, or ends up feeling embarrassed and foolish. Even worse, if you lost your temper over a minor irritation that was nobody's fault and then realised later you were being stupid, it could ruin the rest of your day. The truth is that even though your complaint may have been justifiable, *you* become the victim, not the other party. How can you prevent this from happening?

1. Work on detaching yourself emotionally from the upsetting trivia of life. Tell yourself over and over again that 'big' people handle little irritations gracefully.

2. Train yourself to look beyond such incidents. One way to accomplish this is to walk away from the irritation, reminding yourself that life is too short to worry about minor annoyances. There are more important things to do.

3. Quickly ask yourself, 'Who will be the victim?'

AGREE	DISAGREE	UNCERTAIN
☐	☐	☐

Technique 5
Recognise warning signals

Most people wear blinkers when it comes to being victimised by others. Their feelings get hurt; they blame the other person and react without considering the long-term consequences. Some people follow this pattern over and over again.

How can you learn to warn yourself before you do excessive damage to an important relationship?

The first step is to ask the questions:

- Do I have more to lose than the other person?
- Is there still a chance of salvaging the relationship?
- Is open communication still a possibility?

The best early warning signal is to be aware of your own attitude. Are you starting to react negatively to a person or situation? Are you as positive about your career and your work situation as you were previously?

> On his last formal assessment, Roger was given a 'satisfactory' rating for attitude. His previous rating had been 'above average'. When Roger asked why, he was told that his enthusiasm and consideration for others seemed to have diminished measurably. Thinking back to a relationship problem that had occurred in his department, Roger acknowledged that this was when he had started to adopt a negative attitude and that the change in rating was justified.

Everyone is in charge of his or her attitude. You cannot expect others to tell you when it turns from positive to negative. But if you are honest and in tune with yourself, you will know when it happens. When you sense that things are out of tune, ask yourself why you feel that way and then try to turn things round. Your negative attitude may be the best signal you have to begin rebuilding a relationship before it is too late.

AGREE	DISAGREE	UNCERTAIN
☐	☐	☐

Technique 6
Choose advisers carefully

When a dispute arises it is important to talk things over with someone who is objective. It is also therapeutic to do this. But whom should you choose? And on what basis?

Common sense tells us that it is advisable to keep home problems away from work and some work problems away from home. This is especially true when you need to discuss a conflict involving a colleague or family member. For example, unless you have an outstanding relationship, it is probably best to talk over a serious disagreement at work with a mature outsider (spouse, friend, or professional counsellor.) On the other hand, talking freely about a home problem with a colleague may harm your work output, your image, or possibly cause an upset at home, especially if word gets back that you have been discussing details of your private life.

Either way, the problem is to find the right person to advise you, someone who can be objective. Those closest to you may be your logical first choice, but if they are not objective, taking their advice could do more harm than good.

When Julie had a home problem, her two best friends at work tried to offer advice based on their own experiences. Julie welcomed their support, but it only aggravated the situation at home and interfered with her work performance. The delay (eventually Julie found a solution through professional help) damaged her ability to concentrate at work.

So what is the answer?

Discretion!

Choose your confidantes carefully so your problem will not spill over and upset other relationships at home or at work. The following suggestions may help.

1. Select an adviser who understands the self-victimisation concept and is far enough removed from the problem to be objective.

2. Try not to settle for any advice unless both parties in the conflict stand a chance of coming out on top.

3. Be true to yourself and your judgement.

4. If you asked a friend for advice, consider the help you received as a favour and try to return it in the future.

AGREE	DISAGREE	UNCERTAIN
☐	☐	☐

Technique 7
Distance yourself

When a relationship is important to your career, you must use good communication to resolve any conflict that might arise. But what do you do when you see trouble ahead from someone who is only interested in what he or she can get out of it and doesn't really care about you?

In recent weeks Janet has become aware that her colleague Alan has been using her to further his career. He interrupts her work to ask about things he should be learning in his own time. He asks her to cover for him while he is playing office politics elsewhere. He is generous in buying drinks after work, but almost all the conversation is directed towards subjects that will further his career, not hers. Slowly, Janet has decided that their relationship is never going to be mutually rewarding.

Already a victim, how can Janet stop the process from continuing or getting worse?

Withdrawing from any relationship (instead of trying to resolve the conflict) is sometimes a mixed blessing. This is because the relationship is probably satisfying some need or the person who is the victim would have got out sooner. 'Distancing' is a technique in itself. The following tips may help:

1. Go about it slowly even though your fellow-worker may suspect what is happening.

2. Play it clever in human relations terms by becoming more involved with other colleagues so that other relationships are strengthened.

3. Consider changing lunch and after work habits so you will have less contact with the individual concerned.

Not all relationship conflicts with fellow-workers can be resolved. Doing nothing when you know that the victimisation process is operating is not good enough. You must learn to distance yourself.

AGREE	DISAGREE	UNCERTAIN
☐	☐	☐

Technique 8
When to compromise

If you react to any upset by adopting an eye for an eye philosophy, you will quickly victimise yourself by upsetting other people as well. Your aim should be either to leave the other party alone or help that person win (even if he or she started the dispute) because it is the only way *you* can win.

> When David heard that Thelma was getting the promotion he expected, his first reaction was to tell his colleagues that she was a poor choice. Then, realising that this 'sour grapes' approach would show him in a bad light in front of the others, David changed his mind. Two months later he received a promotion better suited to his talents. Both he and Thelma came out ahead.

Compromising in order to protect our future without hurting others is good human relations policy for many reasons. Here are two:

1. Conflicts that hurt others can have a boomerang effect if management senses productivity has been lowered.

2. Vindictive behaviour is never respected by others.

Sometimes compromise is best for the following reasons:

1. It can generate new rewards that are as valuable or more valuable than those that are lost.

2. When you accept new ideas in the course of a compromise, you benefit.

3. Compromise may be the *only* way to repair a relationship.

AGREE	**DISAGREE**	**UNCERTAIN**
☐	☐	☐

Technique 9
Have 'Plan B' ready

There are two basic ways in which you can become a career victim in today's world.

1. You can become a casualty as the result of a human relations problem left unsolved.

2. You can become a victim because of an organisational change.

As an insurance against either possibility you should have an alternative career option known as 'Plan B'.

Human relations problems are covered in this book. Organisational changes are not, but they are more frequent today than ever before. Mergers, cutting down, restructuring, and technological advances have increased the intensity of the winds of change. Job security can no longer be assured. Even with the correct attitude to human relations, outside influences have the potential to cause problems that may make a career change necessary or advisable.

What is Plan B? It is simply a thoughtful strategy that can be put into action on the day you decide on a career change. A professional Plan B is a systematic thought-out plan of action for furthering your career that includes the following steps. It:

1. Ensures that you are as efficient as possible in your present job (Plan A).

2. Keeps your job skills up to date so that your marketability is maintained.

3. Includes keeping a positive eye open for other, potentially better, opportunities.

Because there are always conflicts in relationships and the winds of organisational change will continue to blow even harder, experts today are saying that a career Plan B is a necessity, not an option.

AGREE	DISAGREE	UNCERTAIN
☐	☐	☐

Technique 10
Your attitude is priceless: protect it!

Most employees are keen to do a job well. Their positive, cooperative attitude contributes to their output as well as that of their colleagues. Mature people realise that when their attitude becomes negative, this is a signal for trouble ahead, including self-victimisation.

Readers who are 'attitude conscious' are aware of the negative consequences for their careers which a poor attitude can bring. They know it is their personal responsibility to stay as forward-looking and productive as possible, no matter what their home or work problems may be. To help you to stay positive, the following techniques are taken from the book *How to Develop a Positive Attitude*.

1. Use the 'turnover' technique

When confronted by an irritating problem, turn it over to see if you can find something funny that will soften the blow.

> When Richard discovered someone had dented his bumper in the staff car park he laughingly announced that he would buy the culprit a drink if his or her insurance would help him to buy the new car he was already thinking of getting.

This technique (even if you don't find anything amusing) may keep you from turning yourself into a victim.

2. Play your winners

The idea is to concentrate on the good things so that the bad ones seem smaller by comparison.

> When she had a problem with her supervisor, Melissa kept herself in a good frame of mind by writing down a positive factor about her job every time she became upset. After exhausting all the positive things she could think of (seven) she decided her job was better than she had thought, so she organised a meeting with her supervisor to see if things could be improved through better communication.

3. Insulate yourself against major worries

When a major problem starts to upset you, it is psychologically possible to push it to the perimeter of your mind so it won't interfere with your productivity.

> Dolores, a popular and respected worker, had to take a week off when her only son was severely injured in an accident. Upon her return, she forced herself to think 'work' instead of 'hospital' and discovered it really helped her to get through that difficult period.

4. Share your positive attitude with others

Doing something special for another person is the best way to shake off negative feelings.

Six months ago when a family problem caused Will to feel lethargic at work, he managed to get over it by doing something special for a different person at work each day. Most of the time it was nothing more than a friendly compliment or an appropriate joke. Now Will maintains his positive attitude by continuing to behave in the same way.

5. Improve your image

One way to fight back when you have been a victim (or you feel negative) is to improve your image.

When Yvonne allowed her attitude to deteriorate during a flat period that she had not anticipated, she restored it by creating a new image through a change of hairstyle, new clothes and dieting. When sales improved in her organisation, she was immediately promoted.

When it comes to winning at human relations, attitude is your most priceless possession. Anything you can do to keep it consistently positive is a good investment.

AGREE	DISAGREE	UNCERTAIN
☐	☐	☐

CHAPTER 5
Final Review

Six questions and answers

1. *When it comes to human relations, it seems to me that an ounce of prevention is worth a pound of cure. Am I right?*
Absolutely! Once the self-victimisation process starts it is difficult to stop it. Therefore, the better you become at maintaining relationships the fewer conflicts you will be forced to deal with.

2. *Won't the passage of time cause some working relationship problems to disappear without action from either party?*
Not always. Even when it happens, a great deal of distress and loss of productivity can take place until time pushes the conflict into the distance. Open communication at the beginning can often prevent this from happening.

3. *What kind of commitment is necessary to win at human relations?*
A sincere, determined, three-part commitment! First, continue to improve your human relations skills. Second, use Mutual Reward Theory to restore any broken relationships. Third, recognise that the moment you lose your positive attitude you are victimising yourself.

4. *Is it possible for someone to remain sufficiently positive when there are long-term problems at home so colleagues will not know what is going on?*
When outside problems are severe, they usually have an impact on job performance. That is one reason why it might be an idea to seek psychological counselling (with the support of management).

5. *If you are not used to confronting people who are trying to victimise you, won't such a step take an emotional toll?*
On a temporary basis, yes. But the damage from allowing an intimidating relationship to continue could be far greater. Another advantage is that it probably will not be so difficult (or damaging) the next time it is necessary.

6. *When is enough enough? When should a conflict cause an individual to pack up and leave a job or organisation?*
Once the victimisation process between a superior and a worker reaches an advanced stage, it may be time to seek a transfer or look to another firm. A conflict between two fellow-workers may not require such a drastic step. All this assumes that attempts at restoration have been made.

Test yourself

Demonstrate that you are good at human relations by answering true or false to the following questions. (Correct answers will be found at the end of the exercise.)

True False

_____ _____ 1. The challenge in this book is to make the most of human relationships without becoming a a victim.

_____ _____ 2. Most people automatically know how to balance their technical and human relations skills.

_____ _____ 3. One can be more objective dealing directly with personalities than concentrating on the relationship.

_____ _____ 4. A mutually rewarding relationship is one where both parties receive more or less equal, but different, benefits.

_____ _____ 5. A 'conflict point' in a relationship can occur when one side gives or receives too many 'rewards'.

True False

_____ _____   6. MRT is a poor approach to use in mending a damaged relationship.

_____ _____   7. Fortunately, the attitude of one employee does not influence the productivity of another.

_____ _____   8. The key to restoring any damaged relationship is the willingness of both parties to try.

_____ _____   9. The decision as to whether or not to try and repair a damaged relationship depends on who was at fault.

_____ _____ 10. People who are adept at human relations never become victims themselves.

_____ _____ 11. Embarrassing yourself in public does not come under the category of self-victimisation.

_____ _____ 12. Employees often become victims when they don't mend a reparable relationship quickly.

_____ _____ 13. The more important a relationship the less likely one is to be a victim.

_____ _____ 14. Standing on principle does not involve risks to human relationships.

_____ _____ 15. Business partnerships create few victims.

_____ _____ 16. Self-victimisation usually occurs when one cannot handle the emotional strain that goes with a relationship conflict.

_____ _____ 17. Absenteeism seldom leads one to become a career victim.

_____ _____ 18. When it comes to a severely damaged relationship within an organisation, it is always best to cut your losses and start again elsewhere.

_____ _____ 19. Plan B can be designed to help you from becoming the victim of an organisation.

_____ _____ 20. Signs of a negative attitude may be an early warning that one is being victimised.

Answers
1. T; 2. F; 3. F; 4. T; 5. F; 6. F; 7. F; 8. T; 9. F; 10. F; 11. F; 12. T;
13. F; 14. F; 15. F; 16. T; 17. F; 18. F; 19. T; 20. T.

Suggested answers to case studies

1. Jeff and his boss (page 12)

Jeff has too much invested with his firm not to give the suggestion a serious try. If he resigns or takes early retirement, he
could be victimising himself while his boss gets away with it.
Once Jeff stops talking about the irritating characteristics of
his boss (and reinforcing them in his mind), he will be better
able to concentrate on his responsibilities. This, in turn, will
be therapeutic. The relationship between Jeff and his boss
may never be fully repaired, but by becoming more objective,
Jeff should be able to survive without too much emotional
stress until normal personnel changes eliminate the problem.
Jeff is already a victim but his actions could alter the balance
and restore the upward mobility of his career.

2. Jennifer's image (page 21)

Although difficult, open communication with Vicky from the
outset could have kept the working and social relationships
separate. Professional employees do this succesfully all the
time. Inexperience with people was probably the reason it
took Jennifer so long to catch on. In most work environments
it is impossible for a high-productivity employee to 'carry'
a low-productivity employee without damaging her or his
image and career progress.

3. Relationship reversal (page 34)

Sometimes a positive approach to a potential relationship
conflict is the only way to keep from being victimised. Mr
Johnson may have saved his career by taking early action. His
wife is to be complimented for her insight in recommending
the MRT approach.

4. William and Philip (page 36)

To protect their careers, non-assertive people like William need to train themselves to stand up to confrontations without making victims of themselves. The fact that, in the USA, eight-hour seminars are often devoted to the process indicates that it is not an easy one to learn. The following pattern might help William to get started: (1) Discuss the situation with an objective adviser who is more experienced in confrontations. (2) With the help of this person, draw up a plan to minimise the possibility of further conflict. (3) Carry out this plan calmly without malice or vindictiveness. (4) Whatever happens, try not to take things personally. (5) Return to the original adviser for an assessment of results so that improvements continue.

5. The vulnerable professor (page 47)

Early and open communication between Dr Franklin and his assistant could have resolved their philosophical differences before they reached conflict point and spilled over to the students. Dr Franklin should have taken the initiative. The MRT approach could have resolved the conflict. Yes, it is a fair statement to say that Dr Franklin victimised himself. He should have reminded himself that communication is the life-blood of any relationship and taken the first step.

6. Disposable relationships (page 51)

It looks as though Helen has become jaded about human relations and, as a result, she may have been too hard on Denise. Many people become human relations victims over and over again without becoming hardened, insensitive or recluses. Helen sounds as if she still carries the scars of past victimisations with her.

Further Reading from Kogan Page

Don't Do. Delegate! James M Jenks and John M Kelly, 1987
Effective Interviewing, John Fletcher, 1988
Essential Management Checklists, Jeffrey P Davidson, 1987
The First-Time Manager, M J Morris, 1988
How To Be an Even Better Manager, Michael Armstrong, 1988
How to Develop Your Personal Management Skills, Jane Allan, 1989
How to Make Meetings Work, Malcolm Peel, 1988
How to Solve Your People Problems, Jane Allen, 1989
Profits from Improved Productivity, Fiona Halse and John Humphrey, 1988
Readymade Interview Questions, Malcolm Peel, 1988
Winning Strategies for Managing People, Robert Irwin and Rita Wolenik, 1986

Better Management Skills

Effective Meeting Skills: How to Make Meetings More Productive, Marion E Haynes
Effective Performance Appraisals, Robert B Maddux
Effective Presentation Skills, Steve Mandel
The Fifty-Minute Supervisor: A Guide for the Newly Promoted, Elwood N Chapman
How to Communicate Effectively, Bert Decker
How to Develop a Positive Attitude, Elwood N Chapman
How to Motivate People, Twyla Dell
Make Every Minute Count: How to Manage Your Time Effectively, Marion E Haynes
Managing Disagreement Constructively, Herbert S Kindler
Successful Negotiation, Robert B Maddux
Team Building: An Exercise in Leadership, Robert B Maddux